Follow the Stag and Learn to Fly

Anna Percy

Follow the Stag and Learn to Fly

Anna Percy

Three Drops Press
Sheffield, England

First published in 2016 by Three Drops Press

Three Drops Press
Sheffield, United Kingdom

www.threedropspoetry.co.uk

Three Drops Press is an independent imprint of Endaxi Press.

ISBN 978-1-907375-33-0

Cover art: 'Stag Lady' by Sarah Peploe © Sarah Peploe 2016.

Thank you to my parents: for filling the house with books, my step father for speaking poems he carried in his head from childhood aloud, my mother for making her own fairy stories and showing me how to be a writer

My legs are an Ocean

you are most of my length and rightly admired
even down to the too narrow ankles

you look dazzling in fishnets you are
sinuous as a mermaid's tail

you are a siren call with your thighs
you have been known to entrap men like seaweed
you dance like a wave full of jellyfish
you are the pull of the tide

The Abyss

There are hidden treasures in this deep fishes with no name merpeople and things with so many eyes and whiskery protrusions you cannot count. Some make jewels part of the shells hermit crabs and their ilk are known to scuttle off with a tiara and build a sparking carapace before discarding the whole thing to the depths. The wrecks are subsumed by the merpeople like the hermit crab into their palaces. There are hulking wrecks of steel twisted into beautiful towers and Elizabethan oak bellied vessels form vaulted ceilings. They laugh at the figure heads simulation of merpeople the breasts and lurid paint work amuse them they place them in galleries for them all to laugh. There are not many now who rise up above the surface for long the new ships are too fast submarines gave them a fright until they realised they could not reach their glittering junk palaces. The pressure too great from anything made by man they never seem to reach that depth remain many fathoms above and still debris rains down. They do not distinguish between televisions and diamonds all are precious objects and fashioned into something useful. Twisted by their hands and tails and the depth pressure into stair cases they have no need of windows use portholes as decoration they make tiaras from silver spoons and keys they find watches smashed, stopped some kind of beautiful moon-shaped mystery. There is no sound that you or I would hear they pull percussion from oil drums and feel the vibrations to dance in their aquatic way, make xylophones from the ribs of the bodies of humans decayed by salt water. They have no reverence for our dead they are merely calciferous as coral.

We are our Own Muses

We are basking sharks in the Lochranza whisky glow of our shared verse and kinship and I feel us three women, poets, myth weavers are writing our true selves after years of word stumbles spooling lines out like kites high wire truths that cross like lightning. Together we are turning over the shells that hide our seal courage. We lift our vinyl crack voices to the sea and watch our black dogs miniaturise and scurry in the surf.

Charmless

I would create a truly useful charm
a charm against charm
I could have used it more than once
a clear magnifying glass to expose charlatans
I would give it you in a locket
to wear over the heart to remind you
it will test the purity of others hearts.

Follow the Stag

he has hung stars
from his antlers
he has leapt up
and pierced the sky
his antlers are stained
with stardust
he is as silhouette
as the leaping stag
on the road sign
on laminated signs
beware the sign of the stag
beware the stag
be aware of the stag
be wary of the false stags
and their fake stardust
glitter is not stardust
find the stag trailing
stardust in its wake
and using it to hover over lakes
rake up the dropped stardust
and learn to fly

For Sylvia

The mirror is a lake sudden and enormous
a flat surface teeming with life underneath
she can name you all the fishes and crustaceans
not shirk from their telescopic eyes as I would
She dwells either in twilight or scorching sun
perched on a rock an anomaly in a striped two piece
sobbing and holding a red balloon she hides a blade   under a shell
scents bladder wrack, kelp, candy floss, cotton candy to her
beaches smell the same in all hemispheres
A white hot day where sand startles the eye reflective
she will reside like a mermaid until she shivers
waiting for the rising of her familiar companion
she traverses night terrors anchored to the moon

Narcissus is in the 27 Club

Narcissus is the main attraction now
Our obsession with beautiful deaths
The beauteous youths who never wither
Now more than ever,
Dali focused on the body calcified it in paint

And now we come to
Those new photos released of Kurt's room
The police on the scene posed like they knew
This would make its way into the papers
A small unit of fame for having been near
the beauty and its end

Echo is pushed out forgotten
Not even given others words to speak
The myths love women's silence
Transforming them to animals
Or inanimate objects burning them up
Now we transform women who speak
Out, up, express their opinions they become
Disfigured by insults silenced by threats to their body

Lochranza Churchyard

The dangerous graves have been reclaimed
by the boggy earth
the angels have lost their heads
and all messages are obscured by lichen
many are lost at sea
the weather wears down monuments fast
the sea makes time more sudden
the robins remind us of this

The sold glamour of looking

eat me
whatever split
too close take care
beware of angels
beauty a fine line
a buried giant
most desired essence
Oh you mango
forget behind
scoop out of shade
island for an aura
whatever the pleasures
strictly I was golden from love heat
victory bluntly love dresses me
who apart cares the pretty bottle
my man with everything says
nice fun to see the life

We Could Be Merpeople (Just For One Day)

When our pens fail take me with you to the canal,
I will tell you where I hid the tails a fin secret
for just such an occasion when we were at an low ebb
we will make beds of discarded shopping trolleys
bouncy balls will be our erratic pearls
wear crisp packet tiaras and beer can finery,
we will sing haunting songs under bridges
taking the rattle of train tracks as our bass
make flutes from bent piping
lure those who are lost to join us
with our beautiful off key music
and as the sun sets we will shake off the fading scales
clamber back to land on unsteady feet

Undergrowth

This could be myth
change the location
time period
the age of the protagonist
a maiden found confused
in the undergrowth
we could skew reality
I knew the trick once
make her more beguiling
beautiful trouble
is more worthy of sympathy
she could be someone
travelled from far away
this world she has found
herself in lacks any sense
that she can make of it
we could make poetry
of her situation, whimsical
people like that rarely
incur repercussions, harm
the facts startle me
into childhood fiction of her

Nocturne

Last night I dreamed she broke in
she'd know how to elbow a window
dreams erase the need for ladders
she took the notebooks from my shelves
although we haven't spoken in years
I conjured her mocking tones wholesale
vitriol distorted by distance and sleep
She tore off strips of my scrawl vicious
rolling them up with great ceremony
in my nocturnal subconscious
she did what she always did on waking
while laughing she ate my words

"She's a Landmark of America"
(After The Patti Smith Poem Title)

She has never apologised for taking up space, for existing, for her cunt, for her hair, her flashing eyes that see you and know your flawed heart and the hurt you have wished on women. She is an illusion in your mind she is tall as a sky scraper she is a stone oracle carved in a modernist style she encroaches on the skyline she pierces the smog with her searchlight, eyes her breath is the wind. She would bend and swallow you and your whole lousy street. She is there on a bench human sized and enormous an eyelid blink between the two monument and woman who is emboldened by her decades of surviving you will never know if you are inspiration for a poem or song or muck in her all seeing eyes. You find your confidence killed by the set of her shoulders, the shrugs she gives her body could be home to you fortress of comfort it could be a bemoated castle you desire her kind looks.

The Cave of My Sane Mind

There is the damp air a strange comfort
Something easier to breathe
A breathing space of a cave
The place where anxiety recedes

"a woman like that causes her own trouble"

That voice cannot follow me into the caves
All the voices stop I am safe to hibernate
That fizzing energy which animates me
Beyond sleep and fatigue is quelled

"a woman like that talks too loud"

I can stop my mouth running off running over
Those words that spill too freely stopped up
There is no need of speech here

"a woman like that makes men feel bad"

The inequities that exist are pushed out by the warm air
By my own hot breath find a space where nothing can hurt
And I am free to think slowly and gently.

I'm intoxicating

I am the strongest liquor you have ever sipped
watch out don't glug I might burn your lips

there's something sweet like honey, like honey
a reminder of summer roses
then sharp aniseed

I can be cloying
many will need to take small measures
we provide a thimble with each bottle
others will find the need to cut me with ice
with soda water to thin and cool my effects

your first taste will shock your tongue
and by the third you're hooked

your first bottle won't be your last
you will thirst for me like no other

A Poem in Spite of Things

The upstairs flat's bathroom has sprung two leaks again
wakes me at six I clutch my books away from the lines
and later at the university water falls from up above
I can only think I am an urban water nymph and my
volume of tears has brought forth water from plaster
cycling here the rain from the sky which lightly misted
as it warmed on my face it fell and joined the fog

Selkie

We watched for months
heard from those who
found their skins in chests
locked away

I learned that locks require a key
to open cleanly
like an oyster revealing the pearl
of your stolen hide

when a chest washed ashore
salt stained with a key half turned
I took my chance
we had seen him
the one who stole your pelt

made you work for him
mop his floors
you showed me this with your
fins and seaweed at low tide
the hours you spent
in his house far from waves

I struggled to tell them apart at first
their fur patched on certain parts
you taught me
the colours and shapes of man

I whipped off my skin
quick as he taught you to gut a fish
you kept watch safe in fur
with your marble eyes
I buried my skin, my return ticket
wanted on voyage in the creaking chest
deep in the damp sand

we'd dug up a dress
you told me where to put my head
such a loose unconnected skin
I staggered across the dunes
marram grass whipping
my new sensitive surfaces
to exact your revenge

Girl

she is made of bus tickets
leaky pens, bottle caps
and love poems written
only to attract love

she dances strange steps
that conjure a beat
and her voice when she
found it was vinyl crackle

she is smudged eyeliner
graffiti in toilets that
tells you that you are beautiful
when your tights are laddered

you have always been a real girl
made of important discarded thoughts

I, Monster

I knew I was something of a monster as a child when in the mirror I felt a changeling, I played with it then as I grew the mirror became a tricky liminal space where I forgot myself and my face, this is dissociation. I knew as I grew and my mind caused me to stop making sense told my tears were crocodile and my rages were funny I didn't know what it meant to be bipolar could not have picked my symptoms out, I had only the Bell Jar to compare myself I reread it again and again repeated the mantra "if I am not as mad as her I am ok" I had only a binary of sane and mad, the mantra began to fail. I knew that something was making me other as my body shrank and my vision buzzed and dissolved as sleep evaded me I could drink vodka and eat nothing and stay up all night and day reality fell away. After I left the hospital I was made to feel a monster by many monstrous unpredictable at best a burden some who were as confused as I or patient knew I had no mask I was not their monster I wasn't hiding something violent. Sill now my psychosis, I thought I was psychic, the loss of all my faculties the way I clawed my way back and still sometimes see hear taste and touch what isn't there makes me feel monstrous I know about the monster when people won't believe my diagnosis they are scared of what it means

I knew I was a monster at seventeen, misdiagnosed with Dissociative Identity Disorder or multiple personalities as these were brought forth I only ever saw people with it on horror movies, a dozen alibis built in a nail biting plot twist and never a human with trauma or on a documentary heavy on the pity. Though I lost the ability to read and write and make any sense the psychosis brought a sick relief I was given a smaller monster, bipolar can be leashed by medication or so the tale goes

I have often tried to make lovers or friends see the monster I have known under my human mask test their loyalty am I really your beloved monster? Can you love someone as monstrous as me?

when the media makes us monstrous we fail to recognise our illness
and that is all we are given to believe we are

every time I tell my story I feel less monstrous.

Acknowledgements

Thank you to Flapjack Press for permission to re-publish 'The Cave of My Sane Mind' and 'Nocturne', which originally appeared in *Lustful Feminist Killjoys* by Anna Percy and Rebecca Audra Smith (Flapjack Press, 2016)

Other books from Three Drops Press

Constellations by Susan Castillo Street
Under-hedge Dapple by Janet Philo
Back to Yesterday by Zoe Broome
The Unicornskin Drum by Stella Bahin
Among the White Roots by Bethany W Pope

Full Moon & Foxglove: An Anthology of Witches and Witchcraft
Tailfins & Sealskins: An Anthology of Water Lore

Coming soon

There is an island by Johnny Giles
A Sprig of Rowan by Rebecca Gethin
The Darkling Child and Other Stories by Catherine Blackfeather
After the Fall by Cora Greenhill
Lykke and the Nightbird by A.B. Cooper
She who pays the piper by Sue Kindon

A Face in the Mirror, A Hook on the Door: An Anthology of Urban Legends & Modern Folklore

www.ingramcontent.com/pod-product-compliance
Lightning Source LLC
Chambersburg PA
CBHW060552030426
42337CB00019B/3532